I0425125

A True Confession

Copyright © 2010 Michael D. Wood

WHEN

NO ONE

HEARS

A story about my life. How the devil placed a seed inside of me. A seed that grew and manifested itself as a troubled boy. Into a disobedient teen. All the way Into an addicted adult.

How lack of communication with teachers, parents, ministers or anyone. Contributed to effects of the out come. How drugs and alcohol and rock music all played a roll in the scheme of things.

How no one wanted to hear what I had to say. No one cared enough to listen to me.

Copyright © 2010 Michael D. Wood

Chapter 1
A Seed Planted

Chapter 2
The Seed Blooms

Chapter 3
The Seed Becomes A Weed

Chapter 4
The Pulling Of The Weed

Chapter 5
Fresh New Ground

Chapter 1

A Seed Is Planted

I was raised in church. Ever since I was born. All I knew was church and singing. Mom and Dad always went to what some people call a "Spirit Filled Church." That is where the people of the church get caught up in the "Spirit of God".

Sometimes they run, sometimes they scream, sometimes they shiver. Sometimes they would shake their arms as if they were trying to shake off something that had a hold of them. I never fully understood this kind of action. Although people called it "Shouting."

The Bible does speak of this kind of actions. But it does not worship God. In the book of Exodus Chapter 32, verses 1 - 35 tell of how the children of Israel made a false God and worshiped it. Feasting and partying and dancing and music and nakedness. Similar in ways to the way I understand it as the "Spirit filled churches."

When I was little, and a church service began this kind of service. My friends and I would began to cut up, do mischief. We paid no attention at what was going on in the church service. We didn't understand the importance, the significance of it all. All we knew, it was our time to play and have some fun.

On this one night at church service. We had sang and the people were getting excited. Suddenly the whole church was up "Shouting", running around, and Praising God. My friends and I began our routine of mischief.

Now Mom or Dad, if they ever caught us cutting up in church. Well, it was to bad for us when we got home. Both my parents believed fully in sparing the rod. They spared it too, in a big way.

Dad and Mom both had always told me and my brothers. That a church service like the one we had just left from. Was a special service. That God was in the midst of the people. That if we cut up and didn't pay attention. That God could let something bad happen to you.

We just thought it was all just Mom and Dad. Not wanting to sit there with their eyes focused on us all the time. Dad loved picking the guitar when the services were all excited and things.

I never saw my Mom or my Dad react with "Shouting", or running, or shivering or things. They always seemed to be as calm as I was. I never saw them "Slain in the Spirit." That is where people pass out for a few seconds, or minutes, or sometimes the rest of the service.

THAT ALL CHANGED FOR ME ONE CHURCH SERVICE.

Although I was raised in church. At home was a different story. There never really seemed to be real true love. Only obligations, duties. My sister and my two youngest brothers were still in diapers and always needing attention. Plus Mom and Dad both worked at the mill.

Mom was always busy with house work. Cooking and feeding us all. Dad was always busy with fixing something. Or teaching us boys a new song to sing. Or just practicing our normal songs.

Although every time we set down to dinner. Dad always prayed and thanked God for the food we were about to eat. I remember Mom had this very old family Bible. It had some amazing pictures in it.

Pictures of Daniel in the lions den. Jesus on the cross. Samson, among a lot of others. I used to love to get that Bible and look and fantasize about what it was like back in them days.

Mom and Dad never did show much affection for us children. Only my sister. I never understood that. I guess it was because she was the only girl born in the family.

I have never seen my Mom and Dad hold hands, kiss or hug, Never. Not even up to this day. I did hear Mom say one day that, that was suppose to be kept secret between a husband and wife.

Mom nor Dad ever prayed with us children before we went to bed or at anytime. Only once can I remember Dad and Mom praying over or for or with one of us. That was me when I had a bad vision. Mom and Dad just brushed it off as a dream. But it was much more than a dream.

Dad or Mom never read us stories out of the Bible. I didn't even realize that the Bible is full of exciting and interesting stories. Until I was thirty four years old. Oh, I'd hear the Minister preach a sermon on somebody. But I thought he had a Ministers Bible that was different from an ordinary Bible. I didn't know they were all the same.

The Bible, or church, or people of the church or Bible were ever discussed or talked about in our home. Only when we had to go visit a church to sing. Then the only discussion was, "You'd better behave at this church tonight. Or I will take you outside and bust your hind end right in front of everyone there." We all knew Dad meant what he said to.

Things for me were about to take a drastic turn. A turn that even to this day, I don't understand why. How was I chosen? Why was I chosen?

When we got home. We all got ready for bed. I had went to bed before my younger brother. We had to sleep together. Mom and Dad couldn't afford a large home. We lived in a small four room house.

It was made to where you could go all the around the home from room to room. I got into bed and went to sleep. Suddenly, I felt something or someone peering over at me. I opened my eyes and was stunned in horror. IT WAS THE DEVIL!

He looked like a very, very old man. With a huge big nose and red sharp eyes. He had huge hands and very long sharp finger nails. He reached to grab me. I screamed and jumped up out of bed and ran. He ran after me. Trying to catch me. I ran around the house in circles. Going from room to room. All the while the devil was reaching out to grab me. I was screaming for help.

Suddenly Dad caught me as I rounded the corner going from the kitchen to the living room. I was sweating profusely. My heart was beating about a thousand beats a second. I was tired, scared, and in shock.

We didn't have a telephone. But my Dad sent my younger brother to the store which was next door to call the pastor of the church. Wasn't but a few minutes until the pastor got to our house. He just lived out the street from us.

The pastor, Mom and Dad all began to pray over me. I began to calm down. That devil, or demon, or what ever it was, was gone now. But not before he had planted a seed of sin into me.

It took a couple years before that seed grew and manifested itself with-in me. I Started out while visiting my brother at our Maw's home. She had a field in her back yard. Maw would always do anything my brother ask her to do. For awhile we made smoking pipes out of hollow shafts of weeds that grew in the field. And acorns from the oak trees. We would pick the leaves off this weed we called "Rabbit tobacco."

We would sit in the field and smoke like two grown up men. We thought we were grown up. My brother got sick one day off smoking that stuff. Maw said it probably from the acorns. So she went the very next day to the store and got us some rolling papers. They were free anyway.

So I learned very, very young how to roll a cigarette. Wasn't long after that. My brother and I figured out how to get some of ole Ben's liquor. We didn't do that but a couple times. Ole Ben knew. He never said anything. But if we had a kept on stealing his liquor. He would have gotten mad. Then he would have told Dad. That would have been a disaster for me.

Wasn't long after that. I began to slip around and smoke cigarettes. Our Maw even showed my brother and me how to cut the inside of a book out and hide our cigarettes in there where Dad couldn't find them.

I had already began to play hooky from school. But Dad or Mom didn't seem to mind that to much. To them, school interfered with our singing and going to church. The only time anything was said from my parents about playing hooky. Was when my friends would get caught. Then their parents would tell my parents. That caused a little uproar. But only a little.

Dad used to smoke. But he quit when I was about three or four years old. I began to take my lunch money for school and buy cigarettes with it. Sometimes our Maw would buy my brother a pack of cigarettes.

I started my younger brother smoking. We would buy a pack of cigarettes and smoke a couple and then hide the pack. If a dog or rain didn't get them Then we had cigarettes for the next day. But if a dog or the rain got them. Then I would buy another pack the next day.

I remember one day. My younger brother and I had just finished smoking one. We had to go home to eat supper. Dad said, "I smell cigarettes. Have you been smoking?" I said no. It probably came from the men at the store.

There was a store we liked to hang around at. It had a pool table and some game machines, (Flipper Machines). The owner of the store at one time was a professional guitar picker for a famous band.

I can't remember the name of the band but I know it to be true. But the owner of the store went blind and could no longer get around by himself. So he stopped playing in the band and bought a store. That really scared my younger brother and me. We almost got caught.

I loved to go stay all night at my Grandma's home. Just to get away from all the rules and regulations of my parents home. All the strictness. All the pressures. At my Grandma's I didn't have any rules. I could voice my opinion, and it didn't matter about what.

Plus my Grandpa smoked cigarettes. He would give me one or two. Sometimes even more than that. They never told my Dad about anything I had ever said. About anything. They never told my Dad about my smoking cigarettes.

I remember one day my younger brother and I were going to the city pool to swim. We had some cigarettes hidden at the rail road tracks. By this time Dad had already figured out we were smoking. He just hadn't caught up to us as of yet.

He was standing in the front yard. He saw us when we stopped and got the cigarettes. He got in his car and slowly drove down to get us. We were caught red handed. Dad took us back to the house. He beat the living tar out of me.

I remember once the belt he was using came across my neck and shoulder. It brought up a huge red and blue whelp. I had huge belt marks all over my back and legs. But that wasn't even the extent to it all.

Dad made my brother and me get into the car. He drove us to the swimming pool. He waited outside in the car. Until we came out around the fence where he could see that we went in. He humiliated us that day. So he thought.

People at the pool could not believe what he had done to us. After Dad drove away. I went back inside to the dressing room. You had to come in and go out through the dressing room.

I sat there the whole time we were at the pool that day. Must have been about three or four hours. I didn't want anyone to see me. I was so embarrassed. I certainly didn't want the girls to see me that way.

I firmly do believe. I deserved some of the whippings I got. Even some of the beatings. But this was one beating I got I didn't deserve.

Mom or Dad couldn't understand what was wrong with me. Neither could I. We as a family never had a close relationship. None of my brothers were ever as close to each other as it is suppose to be. There was never a closeness between me and Mom and Dad.

I guess, having to work in a hot cotton mill all day for little to no pay. Then having to pay what you earn on bills. Then having to worry about our singing and practicing everyday. Just separated us as a loving family.

All us boys were afraid of Dad. We knew how hard he could and would whip us. We also knew Mom would not come to our rescue. All us boys walked a tight rope. We all tried to stay inline as best we could.

Dad always brushed it off as doing as the Bible says to do. I also believe in doing as the Bible says to do. But I have yet to find it in the Bible where the parents are suppose to cast fear and hurt upon the children.

I never hated my Mom or Dad for giving me the whippings and some of the beatings I got. I deserved them. I was an unrulely child. A misbehaved heathen so to speak. I would go from one thing right into another.

I'm not sure how or when it was that I discovered that girls were different from boys. But I do know I liked it. I think I must have been about eleven or twelve years old.

The neighborhood was full of all sorts of different girls. Some tall, some short. Some heavy, some skinny. Some red heads, some blonds. Some with dark hair.

Some were just laid back, family oriented girls. Some were filled with energy. Up and ready for a challenge. Some were sissy fied. Some would beat you up, badly.

All the girls were pretty though. In their own way and being. There was this one girl in particularly, that I secretly liked. When someone was around. I always acted like I didn't like her. Especially when my male friends were around. But deep inside I did like her.

The lady that owned the store about two houses below our home. Began to drive all us children to church. She would have a car full. Sometimes there would be as many as five in the front seat including the driver. There would be as many as six in the back seat.

This certain girl I secretly liked would always end up seated beside each other. I would run my hand up her dress. Into her panties and play with her vagina, on our way to church.

My family had an old one car garage in our back yard. Sometimes this girl would come around after dark. I would be on my home from playing at a friends home. This girl and me would go behind the old garage and I would have sex with her.

I wasn't but about twelve years old. But there was something inside me that would build up a burning desire to do this thing. I liked it, no, I LOVED IT. This went own for a couple years. We never got caught. I was maybe two years older than she was. At twelve and ten years old, can you call that molestation? Or just trying to learn the difference between a boy and a girl.

But those burning, wanting, lustful desires inside me. That I Loved so much. Moved me own to other girls and worse situations.

When I was about thirteen years old. My little sister was about five years old. I really don't know how it all started. But I had gotten to where I would play with her
vagina. It wasn't an everyday thing. Just once in awhile, (seldom).

I remember one night. My sister and I were watching tv. Mom and Dad and my brothers were all in bed. Some how, or some way. We ended up in the kitchen on the floor up against the wall.

She was on top of me and I was playing with her vagina. Suddenly, Dad appears out of no where. He says, "What ya'll doing?" Then he flips on the lights. There we were. Caught red handed.

Dad beat me severely that night. I don't remember if he ever punished my sister or not. We were just young and learning, experimenting, (if you will). A lot of times there were better ways to handle a situation. Other than a whipping, or beating. But My Dad or Mom just couldn't figure that out.

I always said even back when I was little. I would NEVER treat my children so harshly. I will find other means and ways to handle a situation with my children. If I ever grow up and have any.

I always wanted my Mom and my Dad to talk to me. The never did. That was the barrier that separated me from my parents. There was NOTHING I could go them and talk about.

Nothing could I talk to my parents about. I remember one day I went to Dad. I said, "There is this boy at school. He keeps trying to get me to fight him." Dad said, "Well fight him!" That was the end of the conversation.

I could NEVER express my feelings to my parents. My hurts, my desires, my needs, wants or anything. I tried several times. But they always said they don't have time for that right now. Or it'll be ok. Or that they simply didn't want to hear it.

I had a lot of things going on inside of me that I myself couldn't understand or recognize. I was always wanting to do something that I knew was wrong. Something bad. Nothing serious. Just wrong and bad. The urges' inside me were overwhelming.

That all goes back to page 2. All though I was prayed over that night. No one could ever imagine that, that demon or devil had planted a seed inside me. A seed of lust, desire, and mischief.

Mom and Dad didn't want to hear about my feelings. They acted as if they didn't matter. My parents just looked at everything I was doing as just being a boy with problems. Or just a plain ole mean kid.

But really I wasn't just an ole mean kid. I was a kid with problems. Problems that no one seemed to want to hear, or talk about. Not even the school. Although some of the school teachers did see something wrong with me. They never discussed it with me or my parents.

That is when I started to play hooky from school. I always thought that a school was a place of learning. To learn how to cope in the world. To learn how to deal with everyday problems. Learn about life. How to make and live a good life.

I wasn't getting any of that kind of learning from school or my parents. Matter of fact. I wasn't even getting that kind of teaching or learning from the church or Sunday School.

Every time I tried to talk to someone about what was raging inside of me. They just didn't seem interested or care about it. They all seemed to know what my problems was. They all seemed to know just how to handle them. The school would expel me. My parents would beat the daylights out of me. They just didn't know how to make me stop doing the things I would do.

I am here right now to tell everyone first hand. Communication is the key to solving almost every problem a child may have or encounter. When your child tries to tell you something. No matter how strange, or how wild it may seem. No matter how much it doesn't make sense. Listen to them.

Start a good communication with your children when they say their very first words. Keep it going throughout their life. Tell them what is bothering you. How hard your day was at work. How your feeling about your health, finances, or bills. Or just strike up a conversation about something. Clothing, books, cars, anything. Just communicate with your children. Everyday, all day.

Don't judge before you know and have the whole story and facts. Don't make assumptions that you know what is wrong. You may not know.

I ran away from home when I was fourteen years old. I went and stayed at a friends house. I was there about a week or so. Then Dad came and got me. He whipped me for that.

Wasn't long after that. I ran away from home again. I went to a different friends home this time. I was there maybe four days. Then Dad came and got me again. Dad whipped me hard this time.

But I was defiant. I ran away a third time. This time two of my friends were running away from their home as well. We got out on the interstate highway and began to thumb (Hitch Hike) a ride.

We only had our lunch money for our school lunch in our pockets. We never even thought about what were we going to eat the next day. We started out journey around 8:30am that day.

We made it past Charlotte, North Carolina. We made it past Durham, North Carolina. We made it all the way to Halifax, Virginia. It was dark now. Night time had come in. We were hungry and lost.

Suddenly, a Virginia State Trooper pulled over beside us. He knew something was wrong. Three boys ages thirteen to fourteen years old. Out hitch hiking on the interstate highway just wasn't right. He took us up to a Police Station. He tried to talk to us. But we weren't talking.

He gave us some sandwiches to eat and a cold drink. Suddenly, one of the guys got to missing his parents or something. He broke down and told the Officer everything.

Now mind you, my parents were poor as poor could be. I had four brothers plus a sister. Mom and Dad was just a cotton mill worker making about $40.00 a week or so.

This friend called his parents. They said they were on their way to get him. His parents called my parents and my other friends parents as well. They told my parents they would bring me back home for twenty dollars. That is half a weeks pay to my parents. They agreed to pay. So did my other friends parents.

Boy, I didn't want to go home. I knew what was coming when I got there. Dad paid the lady. They left. Man how so desperately I wanted to go with them. Dad beat me hard for that trip.

That was the last time I ever ran away from home. I was never asked why I did it. Neither of the three times I ran away. I was never questioned as to why, or what was I thinking. Nothing.

I had been listening to Rock-N-Roll music for sometime. Dad a lot of times when I would get into trouble. He would say, "It's that no nonsense music your listening to." Deep down inside I knew he was partially right. Rock-N-Roll music is all about rebellion, disloyalty, dishonesty and rejection.

Listening to that stuff everyday, all day, will eventually warp and distort your way of thinking. It will cause you to over react on things. It also will cause you think about things and people and situations totally differently that what they really are.

Rock-N-Roll music causes confusion in people. In their minds. In their hearts. After listening to that stuff for a couple years. I began to think the world was against me. That my parents were against me. That society as a whole was against me.

It made me want to lash out. It made me want to be a nobody. A menus to society. A hard headed heathen. It made me feel and think I was right and everyone else was wrong. Or just didn't understand me or where I was coming from.

It made me want more. More of something. Something I didn't have. But something I wanted and needed to fill the gap. The gap that Rock-N-Roll music left in my very soul and mind.

The more I listened to it. The more I wanted to listen to it. I had a rage inside me. A wanting, needing desire. A craving for something. Rock-N-Roll just fueled that rage. It sparked that wanting, desirous craving that was deep inside my very being.

The more my parents complained about the music I was listening to. The more I wanted to hear. I even started to let my hair get a little longer.

This was a hard thing to do. Dad always cut our hair. He liked it in a military GI fashion. But I began to complain about being the odd ball at school and the neighborhood. I believe Dad began to look around and see all the young boys were wearing long hair at the time. This was one of those very rare and far between occasions when Dad broke soft and said ok.

Things appeared to me as if they were coming along. They were, but not for me. They were coming together for the devil. Rock-N-Roll music was just another device being used by Satan against me.

I was almost sixteen now. I was talking to this American Indian girl. She was so pretty. Her Dad was a full blooded American Indian. But her Mom was an American white woman. She was almost fourteen.

I told my Dad I wanted to marry her. My Dad went berserk. He said, "Are you crazy?". "How are you going to support yourself?" "You don't even have a job!" "Anyway, her parents won't sign for her to marry you."

I told Dad that I had already been talking to her parents about it. They said they would sign for her to marry me. If my Dad would sign for me to marry her.

Dad agreed. So here we all go to South Carolina to sign the necessary paper work. She was about one month away from her fourteenth birthday. I was about two months away from my sixteenth birthday. We got married.

I didn't have a car. So I walked to this company just out the street from where I was living with my new wife's parents. They agreed to give me a job. Even though it was illegal because in the state of North Carolina. You must be at least sixteen to work for a company.

I found out that while I was working. My wife was out running all over town with her sister and their friends. This sparked my mind into thinking all sorts of bad things. Jealously set in.

When I turned sixteen. Dad got me a job where he worked at. Dad gave me some advice one day I have wished a million times over I had a heeded to and took. He told me, "Now when you get your first pay check.

You should take it to the bank to cash it. You need to open you up a savings account. It will only take $10.00. Let the bank take it out right then and deposit it into your savings account. You'll never miss the money. And one day, you'll be glad you did." I just couldn't turn that $10.00 loose. But today, I see what Dad meant. Many times over. I've needed $10.00 to get by on something.

I was working one day. My wife had began to baby sit for this couple. They had a son the same age as my wife, fourteen. Something inside of me told me to get off work and go see what was wrong. So I did.

I went to where my wife was baby sitting. I caught her and this boy having sex. I flew into a rage. He ran away. But I beat her up pretty bad. I made her quit baby sitting.

Dad had a spot of land beside his home. He told me that I could put a mobile home on it if I wanted to. He said that may cure some of the problems I am having as a husband and a married man.

My Dad and myself went looking for a mobile home. We searched for about a week. But no one wanted to make us a good deal. Suddenly, we came upon this mobile home lot. It looked unorganized. Junky and everything looked out of place. Dad said, "I bet we get a good deal her."

So we stopped in and talked to the man. We did get a GREAT deal. A brand new home. Never lived in. Plus they will bring it out, set it all up, free. Plus this guy liked Dad and me for some reason or other.

He threw in on the deal at no extra charge. Thirty foot of sewer line. Two hundred and fifty foot of water pipe. Plus an extra set of storm windows. He also let me keep all the decorations that were in the home for free.

It was a Spanish style home. Black and white decorated tile floors. Black leather living room furniture. Two bedroom, two bath home. It had wrought iron separating the kitchen from the living room. It was beautiful.

But it just didn't seem to impress my wife. We were married about eight months now. I would go to work at 6:00am. Come home at 3:30pm. I would shovel dig ditches by myself to hook up the water and sewer.

I didn't have the money to pay to have the ditches dug. Or to hire some help. I would work on that until dark, everyday. After I got the sewer hooked up. My wife and me moved in with my Mom and Dad.

We ran a drop cord from my parents home to our new home. Most nights my wife and me would stay in our new home. The water ditch I had to dig. Was about three hundred foot long. I had to start out deep, very deep. About eight foot deep.

I had to work my way up gradually as I dug so the water would have a downward force to it.

I had the ditch dug. The pipe was laid. I was going to turn the water on that day when I got home from work. But, that same feeling I once had came rushing back into my mind.

You need to get off work and go home. So I did. Only to find my wife out at my neighbors home. Dancing and running around naked. There were five boys there all different ages. But the youngest one was fourteen. The oldest one was seventeen.

I took her back to our new home. I began to beat her up severely. I flew into a rage like I have never been in before. I believe I might have killed her if she hadn't broke free and ran away.

I made up my mind right then and there. She just wasn't for me. Knowing that two times now I had caught her red handed naked with another boy. This time with a room full of boys.

I lost all interest in the new home now. I didn't never turn the water on. My Dad found a man that would move it and pay for it. So I let it go. From that day until this day. I just have never had another feeling or desire to own a home.

Things like those that happened between my wife and me. Are signs that you can be to young to play the grown up game of marriage. That what you think when your young is love. Is merely just a passing fantasy. It will come to an end sooner or later. We both found out later on. That we had a lot of growing up still to do.

After twenty years or so of not even seeing my ex-wife. One day a letter came for me. It was from her. She wanted me to call her. All sorts of things ran through my mind that day. So I called her.

She was living at the Catawba Indian Reservation in South Carolina. She wanted to meet with me and discuss some things. So we made plans to meet at the store where her Mom works.

Wow, she was still beautiful. She told me she was sorry for the things and the way she had treated me. I told her I was sorry for the way I treated her. We both ask for each others forgiveness. We gave it that day.

I have not heard from her since. I don't try to contact her. I just hope she is happy now. That she has found true love and that true love has found her.

Chapter 2

The Seed Blooms

I was almost seventeen now. I got a car. A job. Some money. I'm single again. I am on top of the world. I got it all. I had been dinking beer for over a year now. One day on the job. I was introduced to some pot, (marijuana). I really liked that stuff. It made me feel different.

A feeling about like being drunk. Except you don't have that full feeling inside like beer gives you. Pot or marijuana made me feel num all over. Num to the work I was having to do. Num to the problems I was having. Num to everything.

I learned as a child. There's is no one gonna help you. No one to discuss the right choices to make. No one to show you a better way to handle a situation. I was on my own.

But it had always been that way. But this pot, this marijuana gave me a new out look on my issues. It made me think I could handle anything that came my way. I thought I had found the cure for my not having anyone to talk to all these years. It made me think it didn't matter. We could handle it.

Wasn't long after that. I was introduced to speed, (Diet pills). Speed and beer works against themselves to cause an imbalance in the mind. Beer wants to put weight on you. While the diet pills want to remove the weight. It confuses the mind and body. Causes a reaction.

I lost weight even though I was drinking beer everyday. I was drinking about eight to ten beers a day at the time. Wasn't long I went from drinking beer to drinking liquor.

When I made the switch. Diet pills stop working for me. That crazy jittery feeling wasn't there any more. I would take two sometimes three diet pills about every two to three hours when I was drinking beer. Now, I was taking five pills every two to three hours drinking liquor.

Then someone introduced me to acid. I didn't know it at the time. But acid is nothing more than rat poison. I didn't care, it made me feel good again. Liquor just seemed to boost the effects of it also.

I was the life's party at work and everywhere I went. Everyone seemed to like me and want to hang around with me. Everyday we got paid at the job I was working at. My friends and my brother who also worked there where I did. We would jump in our cars after work and head to this beer joint in South Carolina.

I had been talking to this married woman. I was almost seventeen. She was thirty five. She and her husband worked where I did. I would take her out in the ware house and we would kiss and play around some. I would feel her vagina. She would feel my penis. We did for awhile. Her husband never knew.

One day while at work. She told her husband she wanted to separate. She told him she wanted him out of her home when she got home that night. So he quit his job and moved out of her home. She would tell me things like, "I am so jealous over you." It made me feel good.

So we started dating openly. My Dad also worked where I did. He got really mad when he found out about me an that woman dating. I said to Dad, "Are you jealous?" he said no. That it just didn't look right. I told him I didn't care what it looked like. I was having fun.

This went on for several months. Then a new girl came to work where I worked at. She was right at my age, and pretty also. I began to talk to her ever chance I got. She was a partier. She like to drink alcohol and beer. She liked to smoke pot. her
Dad didn't seem to mind. He drank beer sometimes himself.

This really upset and made the thirty five year old lady really mad. But I didn't care. Wasn't long after I had met the new girl. The thirty five year old lady quit her job and went away.

The new girl had a boyfriend that worked where I did. We were friends. But at the time I didn't know he and the new girl was dating. Him and me were having lunch one day. I ask him if he had seen the new girl. He told me had, and that she was his girlfriend.

I told him right then and there. "You better watch out for me. I'll take her away from you." He played it off as a joke. But I was as serious as a heart attack. Valentine's Day rolled around.

I went and bought her this huge heart shaped box of candy. I took it to the mill where we all worked at. She was impressed. Her boyfriend didn't even give her a simple card. I had her hook, line and sinker.

But if I had only knew the out come of our relationship. I would have thrown her back.

He got really mad at me and wanted to fist fight me. So we went outside the fence at the mill we worked at. We got it on. He was an ole hard nose plow boy from the country. I was a drunk and drug user. But I was holding my own. Then suddenly the security guard from the mill came out to see what all the commotion was all about. He broke us up.

We never did finish that fight. But he was through with the new girl. I had taken her away from him. But of course, she was done with him also. So me and the new girl began to date.

One day while I was working. Some friends were putting together a party. They invited my new girl. They ask me if I was gong to come party with them I told them I had to work over to get that machine up and running.

My girl went with out me. Later on, it didn't take me as long as I thought it would to fix that machine. So I decided to go on to the party. When I got there. Everyone was in shook. I ask where my girlfriend was at. They told me she had went to the store.

They didn't say with who, or how long she had been gone. Suddenly this one friend of mine came up to me. She said I hate to tell you this. But I think you deserve to know.

You girlfriend left with this boy. They have been gone now for over an hour. Now I had a reputation of fighting and fighting hard. This boy knew me and knew my reputation.

The longer I sat and waited for my girlfriend. The madder I got. People were beginning to see that in me. Soon as the car pulled into the driveway. Some of my friends ran outside and told this boy. I am here and I am mad.

My girlfriend came in to me. This boy drove out the driveway fast. He was scared. I didn't talk much the rest of that night to my girlfriend. I should have seen the signs. I should have heeded the warnings. But I didn't.

I think she may have learned lesson that night also. We dated for some time. She didn't run around on me any more after that night.

My girlfriends Mom got to thinking that her husband was running on her. Which he was. She had seen his car at one of his old girlfriends homes this day. My girlfriends Mom had been spying on that home all day. My girlfriends Dad's car never left.

I was working the evening shift at the mill. That is 3:00pm until 11:00pm. This was on a Friday night. We didn't work at the mill on Saturdays unless it was an emergency. I was living at my Dad's home at this time.

Soon as I pulled into the driveway. Here comes my girlfriend and her Mom. My girlfriend had a big brother who lived in Georgia. My girlfriends Mom told me the story about her husband and this other woman. She ask me if I would drive them to Georgia.

I said, "Sure, why not." So we left right then and there. 11:00pm at night. I didn't even go into the house and tell Dad or anything. I just got out of my car and into my girlfriends Mom's car.

By Saturday evening. My girlfriends Mom had been talking to her husband on the phone. He wanted to talk to me. Now he had a reputation also. Of fighting and cutting people with a knife. He told me he was going to get me for taking his wife and daughter off.

I cussed him out. I told him he knew where i was at. Come own down and get me. I told him if I had my own car, I would meet him half way there. I wasn't afraid of him. Saturday night he called me and apologized. He ask me if I would bring them back home.

I told him not until his daughter and me got married. I hadn't even discussed getting married with my girlfriend. Or anyone else for that matter. He agreed to help us to get married. So that Sunday morning we headed back to North Carolina.

We went that Monday and signed up to be married. There was a three day waiting period. So here comes Thursday. I ask off from work until the following Monday. They said sure. That would be fine.

My girlfriends Dad took us to the mountains. He got us a room and he paid for it all. Our food and all. He never said anything about settling the score about me cussing him out. I guess I impressed him and showed him his daughter wasn't marring a
sissified wimpy ole punk.

There was complete change in my girlfriends Dad after that. Him and some of his friends would get together and make music. They began to go to churches and pick and play.

They went to this one church one night. They had played a couple songs. Most all the members in the band smoked cigarettes. My girlfriends Dad told the church members they were going to take a break and let their fingers rest.

This one church member stood up and made a request for a certain song. She ask if they would play "Mother's Bible." My girlfriends Dad told her they would on the second round. That the band needed to take a break for a few minutes.

They all went outside the church. My girlfriends Dad put a cigarette in his mouth and reached for the cigarette lighter and fell over dead. He had, had a massive heart attack.

Man that was a shocker to me. It was only maybe three months after I married his daughter. The short time I knew him. We got along very well. He never tried to interfere into anything his daughter and me had going on at the time. We lived beside my girlfriends Mom and Dad in the same mobile home park.

It was sad around there for a long, long time. My girlfriends Mom never remarried. She wouldn't even date anyone. She really love my girlfriends Dad.

My girlfriend had this younger brother. He had a monkey for a pet. Just a little ole monkey. A squirrel money I think is what they call them. He turned that thing loose into the trees around where we lived.

Our storm door had a broken window in it. One day my wife had cooked some bread. I came home and opened the door. There was that monkey sitting on the eating table eating that bread. A rage ran through me.

I grabbed the broom and took a swat at that monkey. He jumped and lunged his way out that broken glass window in our door. I was going out to kill that varmint. I reached up and pushed hard on the top glass of that storm door. When I did, that glass broke.

It split my wrist severely. My wife rushed me out to the hospital. They sewed it up. I calmed down while I was at the hospital. I realized that the monkey was only doing what came natural to him.

My wife and me were both drinking alcohol and doing drugs. She was now working for a knitting mill. I had stopped working at the cotton mill and had begun to paint houses. We moved into a mobile home in the country.

I had bought a special edition rifle. A Winchester 30-30. I had been out side shooting it. I thought it was empty. When I came inside the home. My wife was at the sink washing the dishes. Soon as I came in the front door.

I turned to her and said, "I'll just kill you now." I swung the rifle up and all of a sudden. POW! That thing went off. Shooting a hole through the floor about one foot in front of my wife's foot.

It stunned her so badly. All she could do was slide upon the sink and sit there and cry. I was in shock. I threw the rifle on the sofa. I walked directly over to my wife. I put my arms around her and said, "I am sorry. I didn't know it had a bullet in the chamber. I could have sworn it was empty."

I never did try anything like that again to her or anyone else, ever. That taught me a very serious lesson that day. It sobered me up and both my wife and me lost our high from the drugs we were taking at that very instant.

She was pregnant with our first child. We moved farther out into the country. Into another mobile home park. My drinking and doing drugs was beginning to take a toll on me now. I wasn't but about twenty years old. But it had begun for me to get to work on time.

I would blame everything except myself. Now, ever since I was a child. I always wanted a baby boy. Born on my birthday. Well, here comes my first child. A boy, born on my birthday. I felt so special. I was one happy man.

I just didn't understand how to handle all the responsibilities that came with having a child. I was getting fired from my job. Shifting from job to job. Fired here, quitting there.

All I knew was that it wasn't my fault. So I kept telling myself and everyone else. It was the alcohol and drugs. It caused my mind to think differently. It caused my body to act differently. The drugs and alcohol had my mind and body confused. They didn't know how to act or think.

About twenty two months after our first child was born. We had a second child born. This time it was a little girl. My dream as a child was beginning to come real. Just like I had always wanted and dreamed of.

I wasn't able to find steady work anymore. My oldest brother had heard about painting jobs in Texas paying twice the money as North Carolina. So here we go, children and all out to Texas. No plans, no place to live. Nothing except what we could pack into that little Pinto car.

We made it Texas. But it was one more miserable ride. That car didn't have an air conditioner. Crying, hot children, hungry and needing diaper changing. I was hot, drunk, and half way stone.

Looking out for dangerous drivers. watching for road signs and gas stations. The car packed so full of clothes and things. I couldn't even see out the back window. I had to use the side mirrors.

But we made it. Safe and sound. The first night we were there. We stayed in a motel. The very next morning my brother and me went to the paint store. We got a job right off. Now painters in North Carolina at the time were making $5.50 to $6.00an hour. We were offered a job starting out at $9.50 an hour. The boss man told us, "When I see what you can do, your pay will increase."

I don't know how he done it. But after that day working. My brother had found us a house to move into. So there we were. My brother and his wife. Me and my wife and two children. All living in a two bedroom house.

When I got my first pay check. I found my wife an me an apartment. Just up the street from my brothers house. I had met some new friends on the job. They all liked to party and do drugs also.

We would all get together after work everyday and get stoned. All my new friends had children also except two of them. One of them was married but the other one was single.

He said something to me one day about my wife being sexy. I grabbed him around his neck and pulled his face right up against my face. I told him, "Best to get them kind of thoughts about my wife out of your head!" I never had another problem or incident out of him or any of my other friends.

After we had lived in Texas about a year. I came home from work one day. I found a friend of mine sitting on the sofa. I went directly to the bedroom where I found my wife naked trying to get dressed.

I slapped her down onto the bed. I went into the living room and told my friend he had better leave. After about three months my wife was pregnant. I never gave it much thought at the time.

Until my third son was born. He had blond hair. He had a muscular build to himself. I am nothing of that type. Although it was always in the back of my mind. I always tried to hide those thoughts. About my son belonging to someone else.

I never treated him any differently than I did my other two children. When I bought for them I bought for him also. Far as he knows even to this day. Far as anyone knows even to this day. My third son is mine.

I just won't be totally convinced until a DNA test is done. But I love him the same as my other two. After my third son was born. I put them and their Mom on a bus for North Carolina. I stayed in Texas for about six to eight months longer trying to find work and make enough money for me to return to North Carolina.

I had begun to have sex with a friend of mine after my wife was gone. I always felt guilty after we had sex. I never told her that. But I did. She agreed to drive me to North Carolina.

When we arrived. My wife had moved into these apartments. So we drove over there. This girl thought and had the idea that she to was going to be living with me and my wife. She thought my wife was going to share me with her.

Boy was she ever wrong. My wife was about to jump on her. When I stepped in and told my wife, "If it hadn't a been for her. I'd still be stuck out in Texas." The girl left that night going back out to Texas where her family lived.

After a few days I was able to find me some work. The pay had increased since the last time I had worked in North Carolina. That was a good thing I thought. That meant more liquor and more drugs and more parties.

You know what? Drugs and alcohol will over a period of time. Make you a self centered, selfish individual. You soon get to the point where no one or nothing is important to you anymore. Only what You need or only what You want.

My younger brother and my cousin began to come over. They also drank liquor and did drugs. Between their friends and my friends and all of us. We began to party every Friday night all the way into Sunday evening.

I would take my whole pay check and party with it. What I didn't spend on liquor or drugs. I gambled away, playing poker. I even began to take my bill money and gamble it away.

It had become an obsession, a habit. A need that I just had to fill. Just like the alcohol and drugs. I had long ago back in Texas lost any and all affection for my wife. I never even considered my children.

My way of thinking was, well, they have a home and food. If that's not love then what is love? I never bought any new clothes for my children. I never bought them any new toys to play with. My way of thinking was, I didn't have the money for such things. I had to pay a little on the rent, a little on the bills. A lot on alcohol, and a lot on drugs. If anything was left over, that was gambling money then.

All this was taking a toll on my wife. She was working and taking her whole pay check buying groceries, and to finish paying what I didn't pay on the bills. But I never even considered that. I didn't care.

After sometime of this, my wife left me and moved in with her Mom. For about two months I partied hard. But then I began to miss my wife and children. So I went and got them.

I stopped the parties. But I didn't stop the drinking and drugging. But of course my wife also drank alcohol and did drugs. She just didn't do it as much as I did. We moved yet again.

This time it was into a privately owned mobile home. I was around twenty seven or twenty eight at the time. My wife and me had met a new set of friends. They like to Disco dance. They to like to drink alcohol. I introduced them to drugs. They liked them.

One day we went over to our new friends home. They were going dancing. One of our friends didn't want to go at the time. I didn't either really. But my wife wanted to go. So our other friend and his wife said my wife could go with them.

Well, they drove off. My friend and me drank a few beers. Then he said, "Let's go. Well surprise them when we get there." I said, "Ok lets go." So we took off. I drove fast trying to catch up to them. They only had about a thirty minute head start on us.

We weren't able to catch them. When we got to the club. The club was closed due to remodeling. My friend said he might know another club they may have went to. So we drove over to that club. We drove around the parking lot. But was unable to find our friends car. So we returned home.

Around 2:30am I went back to my friends home. My friend told me that his sister and her husband had already returned. I ask about my wife. He said they told him that she had got with someone and left the club before they left.

There is a store across the road that leads to my friends home. So I drove up to the store and parked in the parking lot and waited. Around 4:00am a car turned on the street that my friend lives on. So I cranked my car and slowly crossed the highway and proceeded down the street. The car was coming back out as I was going in.

I pulled up to my friends home. Knocked on the door. They opened up the door. There was my wife laying on the sofa, making out like she had been there all night. I ask her where she had been. She just looked at me. I ask her, "You been with another man?" She said yes. She already knew she had been caught. I ask her, "Did you have sex with him?" She also said yes.

I told her I was going to beat the living hell out of her. I told her I could do it at our friends home and embarrass her or we could take it to the privacy of our own home. She got in the car.

When we got home. i beat her up pretty bad. I told her, "I can't stop you from running around on me. But I can stop you from getting caught." I had busted her head open right above her right eye. It was bleeding bad. So I took her to the hospital. It took five stitches to sew it up.

My wife and me had begun to argue a lot. Over some of the smallest and lest important things. We were losing our love for each other. One Saturday morning.

My wife had to work that day. She drove the car to work. So I walked to up town. I wanted to buy my wife a nice present and surprise her.

I found a really nice dress. I bought it and brought it home. I laid it out on the bed. Where I knew my wife would find it soon as she came from work. Her Mom was there. Well, my wife came in. She went to the bedroom. She came back into the living room.

She didn't seem surprised at all. It stunned her Mom as well as me. I ask my wife, "Didn't you see the dress I bought for you today?" She said. "yes." I ask, "Didn't you like it?" She said, "It is ok."

That rage flew up in me again. I went to the bedroom. Took out my pocket knife and sliced that dress into about a thousand pieces. My wife ask me, "What did you do that for?" I said, "Well you didn't seem to want it. You weren't surprised by it. I just wanted to surprise you today. So I guess I did."

There was another time. Me and my wife had, had a heated argument. She went to work. I began to feel really bad about it. So I went to the florist and bought a nice bouquet of flowers. I took them to her job to surprise her. Her boss man told me he hadn't seen her all day. But the truth was. She was on break sitting in the car with another man. I didn't know that until later on. I just threw the flowers into the trash bend at the door as I turned to walk away.

That seed had me blinded, and deceived as to the way I was. A hard hearted, cold self centered selfish drunk and druggist. All my wife was trying to do. Was reach out to someone for that needed affection. That tender moment of kindness. Someone who would listen to her problems.

It was suppose to be me. But I wasn't capable at the time. I had problems also.

Chapter 3

The Seed

Becomes

A Weed

We moved yet again. I guess we were trying to move and leave our problems behind. But that don't work. Your problems will follow you everywhere you go. Until you solve them.

The stress level was at an all time high now. I was about thirty one years old. My wife had turned into this cold, hateful, grouchy person that I truly didn't like. I kept telling myself, think about the kids. They need you. How will the next man treat them?

Although I wasn't doing anything for my children. How could someone treat them any worse than I was treating them. I really did love my children. I never did have to whip them. I did from time to time have to take my hand and pop their butt. But nothing sever or major. Like my Dad used to do to me.

One day my children were throwing rocks. I told the oldest boy, "Don't be throwing them rocks! You'll break a window and I can't pay for it!" Well, sure enough. After about thirty minutes. Here they all came inside. I could tell something just wasn't right. By the expressions they all had on their faces.

I said to them, "Well you did it, didn't you?" "Broke a window." I always did teach my children not to lie about anything. Even if you knew you was going to get into trouble. Because lying just makes it all that much worse and the punishment that much worse.

My oldest son spoke up and said, "Yes, I broke a window in that old building out back." I told my son, "When the land lord gets home today. You go tell him what you did. Tell him you'll cut his grass or do something to pay for the window."

Well, the land lord gets home. My son like a man walks out to the land lords home. He explains the situation. Next thing I know, here come my son and the land lord. Both crying. The land lord said that is an old building. I was going to tear it down anyway. I just hadn't gotten around to it. Your son don't have to pay for that window.

That was punishment enough I thought for my son. He never threw any more rocks. Matter of fact, none of my children threw any more rocks after that day. So all my children learned a valuable lesson that day.

I remember another time. We had gone to the grocery store to buy some groceries. My daughter wanted me to buy her this make up. I told her no. Well,

We got what we wanted. We paid for it. And then we drove home.

Later on that night. Here comes my daughter into the living room all decorated up with fresh make up on. I said to her, "Where did you get that make up?" She just looked at me. I said to her, "You stole that make up. After I told you I didn't have the money to buy it for you. Didn't you?" She started to cry. I told her to go get the make up and the pack that it came in. That we had to return it to the store.

I told my daughter, "When we get to the store. You take that make up, up to the manager and you tell him you stole that. You tell him your sorry and you promise not to ever steal anything from there anymore."

On our way there. She ask me if she could get into trouble over stealing. I said, "Yes you can. The jails are full of people that steal things." She ask me, "Do you think that manager will put me in jail?" I saw my opportunity, I said, "Well I don't know. He might."

We pulled up to the store. I told my daughter to come on. I got her hand. She had the make up in the other hand. We walked up to the manager. I said, "Now, tell him what you did." All of a sudden she burst out crying. She was trying to tell the manager that she stole that make up. But she couldn't.

I told the manager that she ask me to buy it for her. I wouldn't so she wanted it so bad she stole it. The manager saw how so sorry she was by all her tears. He said that's ok. She can keep it. My daughter was still crying her little eyes out. Almost made me start crying, and the manager also.

This was just a couple of the ways I had vowed to myself as a child. To teach and punish my children totally different than the way I was taught and punished. I didn't have to whip or beat my children. Over some petty mistake they made.

Even though I was a drunk and did drugs. My children loved me. They knew I loved them also. I just had my priorities messed up. I didn't even know what was important anymore.

I had took the children to swim at this creek. My Dad took my brothers and me there when we were little. My Dad's Dad took him and his brothers there when they were little.

We must have gotten there about 2:00pm. My children had already eaten their lunch. So I bought us some soft drinks for when it got really hot. We stayed there until it was getting dark.

My children's Mom was living with this man at the time. When we arrived at my children's home. They told me that their Mom's boyfriend was working a side job and wouldn't be home until after their Mom got home from her job. About 11:30pm.

They ask me if I would go to the store and get them some snacks. I said, "Sure I will." My daughter ask if she could come with me. I said, "Yes." In my mind was a raging war going on.

One thing in my mind was saying, "Here is another chance to have some more fun." Then another thing in my mind was saying, "Now is the time to stop all this before it gets any worse."

I was bound and determined to put a stop to it. I knew this place where drug deals took place an the Police got to where they would watch the place all the time. So I took my daughter there.

I pulled the truck in and we parked. She took of her bathing suit. It was dark. I began to play with her. Suddenly a car turns into the place we were at. My daughter ask me if I wanted her to put her bathing suit back on. I said, "No."

I was desperately hoping it was the Police. It was. Finally it all comes to an end tonight. In the only way I knew how to stop it all. The Policeman questioned my
daughter. Then he told me to follow him up to the Police station.

I could have ran. I didn't have to follow that Policeman. But I did. I didn't want thing to be any worse for me than they already were. I sat in front of the Magistrate's office for what seemed like an eternity.

Wondering what they were doing to my little girl. What kind of questions were they asking her? Is she telling them everything? Is she lying? I didn't know.

They had a doctor come to the jail and examine my daughter. They also got some counselor lady to question my daughter. I guess the whole process took about three hours. All this time I just and waited. Suddenly I saw 2 Policemen coming towards me. I knew I was going to be arrested. So I went to the telephone there on the wall. I called my daughters Mom. I knew she was at home now.

I told her, "Were at the jail house. You need to come get our daughter." That was all I said to her. Then I hung up the phone. That was the last time I saw my daughter for twenty one years. It took nine years for me to see my boys again.

I never wanted to interfere with what they had going on in their lives at the time. I didn't want to cause any more pain or suffering on them than I had already done to them their whole lives so far. Especially to my daughter.

Chapter 4

The Pulling

Of The Weed

The Officers arrested me. They charged me with first degree rape of a minor child. I was placed into jail. Oh, God I thought. What have I done. They placed me under a half a million dollar bond. I was scared. I didn't know what to do.

I began to think, "Did I do the right thing?" "Did I handle it in the right way?" "Could I have done it differently" "What's going to happen to me now?" All these thoughts were filling my mind.

I couldn't eat. I couldn't sleep. All I could think of was the mess I had made. And if I had destroyed my daughters life forever. God was working in the background and I didn't know it or realize it.

The Grand Jury handed down an indictment for me on charges of rape in the first degree. That cut my bond down to one hundred thousand dollars. I didn't care. I felt I was getting everything I deserved. But I also knew in my mind soul and body that I didn't rape my daughter. I had never raped her. I had never even had real sex with her.

Thinking about that began to settle my innards a little bit. Also God was letting me know that He was in control now. Later on I realized I had done the right thing. That I had handled the situation in just the right way that God wanted and intended.

It had been about a month now. I was talking to Mom on the phone. She told me that my case was coming up soon. She also informed me that the counselor that my daughter had. Was taking my daughter to court to watch and see and learn as to what goes on. Mom told me that that counselor had it in for me. Mom told me that I should plead guilty to stop a jury trial and just let it all go with that.

I had already made up my mind to plead guilty on certain charges. But no about rape. Mom told me she had the church and other churches praying for me. That made me feel much better. But I knew with in myself I was guilty for certain things and I didn't expect God to help out a criminal.

BUT BOY WAS I WRONG ABOUT THAT!

God at work. Facing a first degree rape charge. About a week before my trial. Due to the doctors report. My daughter had no signs of penetration. There was no semen. Something inside little girls I don't know what they call it. But little girls when someone like an adult penetrates them. They tear this certain thing inside the girls vagina. My daughters was intact. It had not ever been disturbed.

Based on these facts. A whole new set of charges had to be brought in. The rape charges had to be done away with. I was charged with indecent liberties with a minor child. My bond had to be reset also. It was set at ten thousand dollars.

I could have gotten out of jail and run away if I had a wanted to then. But, I didn't. I wanted help. I wanted to know I would never do that kind of thing again to any of my children or anyone else's children. I was going to stay in jail and get the help I needed.

During this time. My mind had calmed down. My soul had calmed down. I was thinking right and ok again. Suddenly a tune came into my mind. I just couldn't stop humming it. All day everyday. For about a week I hummed this tune. Then suddenly words began to come into my mind.

The words fit the tune I was humming. So I got my paper and pencil out and wrote down the words. Here is what I wrote:

Rescued Me MDW January 1989

On a ship of sin and shame. With the mighty wind and the rain.
I'd lost my sail and rudder in this sea.
It was dark and it was cold. I had nothing to hold.
Dear Lord till You reached right down.
And rescued me.

You rescued me, You rescued me.
You sent your mighty hand down Lord.
And You rescued me.
You picked me up from out of sin.
You put my feet back on the rock again.
You sent Your mighty hand down Lord.
And You rescued me.

I should have known what was in my way.
Before I left that very day.
Dear Lord I'm sorry please rescue me.
I didn't mean to fall from Your care.
That ole devil caught me in his snare.
I'm sorry Lord please set me free.

And You rescued me, You rescued me.
You sent your mighty hand down Lord.
And You rescued me.
You picked me up from out of sin.
You put my feet back on the rock again.
You sent Your mighty hand down Lord.
And You rescued me.

I began to sing that song right in the jail cell. Suddenly another
tune came into my mind. I hummed that tune a couple days. When
all of a sudden words came into my mind again. They fit the new
tune. Here is what I wrote:

Take My Hand MDW 11-07-1989

Take My Hand, precious Lord, lead and guide me.
Take me down the road of life, you lay for me.
Be my light in this life, of bitter darkness.
Light the way, precious Lord, so I might see.

Take My Hand, precious Lord.
The way is dark, the way is long.
Watch out for me dear Lord, I don't go wrong.
Guide my steps, precious Lord.
So I don't stumble.
Take My Hand, precious Lord, to keep me humble.

Take My Hand, precious Lord, so I'll be safe I know.
I'm in the right arms now, just don't let go.
I can see the way clear now.
Thank You God.
If not for You, how far, I would have trod.

Something inside me began to swell up. As I sang the songs
about rescued me and take my hand. I wanted God to rescue me. I
wanted God to take my hand. I had never considered God since
our family band stop going to churches and singing.

I had been missing that so much all through out my years. But the
devil stepped in just at the right time to disrupt God's plans. I began
to pray. Laying on my bed I began to ask God if there was away I
could ever receive His forgiveness. I told God how so sorry I was. I
ask God to not let what I had done to my daughter effect her and
her growth and happiness.

Next thing I knew. I found myself down on my knees beside my
bunk. Tears were streaming down my face. I saw my breakfast try
sitting on the door tray. I had been praying all night and half the
next morning.

When I stood up. I felt so light. Like I could just fly. Something
inside was gone. that pressure, that weight was gone. I felt like a
totally new person. My worries had gone away.

Suddenly a new tune rushed into my mind. I hummed it for about
a couple hours. Then words began to come to me. Here is what it
said:

Whisper In My Ear MDW May 1989

As I lay here late at night.
Looking back at my wrong and my right.
I get a strange funny feeling other than fear.
I know I ran from my God for so long.
Always losing never knowing what's wrong.
Until the day that I heard God whisper in my ear.

I love you, I want you.
Even tho you have ran for so long, I need you.
I miss you, I'll help you.
Was the whisper in my ear that said, "I love you."

When I woke the next day at dawn.
I felt I woke into a new home.
Everything seemed so peaceful, calm, and new.
All my worries had gone away.
My life had changed into a new day.
All because of the whisper that I always knew.

   The dates are wrong on the songs because I reworked the songs
later on. But God was working with me and He was also working
with the court, the charges against me, everything.
   My court appointed attorney came to me about a week before
court day. He said I got you a plea deal. All you got to do is sign it
and be done with it. Now Mom had already told me that if they
offered me a plea deal to sign it. Not to let it go on into court.
   If I had a let in gone on into court. I could have gotten a minimum
of twenty five years. I think the maximum was something like fifty
years. God was still working on my behalf.
   The plea deal was I would plead guilty to indecent liberties with a
minor child. I would get a ten year prison sentence. So I signed it.
About a week after. My case came up before the judge. He gave
me ten years.
   I left the jail in about a week after that. Headed for prison. I had
wrote about six songs now.

I was sent to the Salisbury High Rise. A maximum security prison. When I arrive at the prison. God still wasn't done with me and the people in charge. My ten year sentence was automatically cut to only five years. I could also get time off of that by staying out of trouble. And getting some sort of job to do.

Oh, how so scared I was. That place looked so spooky when we entered the gate. There are people in there with no hopes of ever getting out of prison. Some of the people in there don't even have any hope of living.

One day while I was going to the yard. A man ask me if I had ever killed a man. I said no, have you?. He replied that, that is what he is doing in prison. I could see in his eyes that he didn't have any natural feelings for people or anything. His eyes just looked cold and dark. I was scared.

Another day two people had jumped on a man outside the elevator. They had home made knives. They killed that man. I was on my way to lunch. When I got off the elevator. They had just rushed that man to the hospital. The other two were in custody. Blood was everywhere.

I made it a point to not go anywhere at anytime with out someone with me. I also made it a point not to go anywhere at all except where I had to go. Like the administration office or the cafeteria.

I met some people that were nice there though. Like the barber shop man. He would come and get me on the nights that the churches came to hold a service at the prison. I liked going to the church services.

I wasn't there but two weeks then I was transferred to a medium security prison. It wasn't as dangerous as the maximum security prison was. While I was at the medium security prison. I knew I would be there awhile. So I began to enroll in all the self help classes they offered.

I was also ordered by the judge to go to the DART program. DART stands for Drug Alcohol Recovery Treatment. I also began to take Bible courses. I also got my GED while I was there.

I didn't get a chance to write many songs while I was at the medium security
prison. All the courses I was taking to help myself to never do as I had done ever
again was taking my time away.

I was so desperately wanting to change. I was going to change at all cost. There
were a couple men there. They tried to give me a problem one day. Well, they put
this other man up to doing their dirty work. That man had a mental problem. He
could be talked into anything.

I was taking a shower and this man came in and just punched me. For no reason
at all. The guards just happen to see the whole thing. They rushed in and got the
man. They ask me if I needed to go see the nurse. I said no.

They transferred that man back to the maximum security prison.
Now get this. One of the men who was to afraid to confront me
himself. He was the brother of the Minister who Pastored the church
where my Mom and Dad went every Sunday and Wednesday.

The DART program was a thirty day intense program. I learned a lot about why I
drank and did drugs. But mostly they missed the mark. I didn't drink and do drugs
over trying to settle my problems or issues. I drank and did drugs because I like it.
But I did learn. That drinking and doing drugs will only contribute to the problem.
They only create more problems.

There was a man there at the medium security prison who had a
life sentence. He was never going to get out of prison. He had a
guitar. He would go out to the pick nick tables and pick and play for
hours at a time.

I would go out there and sit and do my work and lessons and listen to him. He
played very well. One day he was coming back in to have a roll call.
He was putting up his guitar. All of a sudden he just fell over dead.
The security officers said he had, had a massive heart attack.

I wasn't at the medium security prison but about eighteen or twenty months.

Then I was transferred to a minimum security prison. I had finished all the self help courses offered by the prison system about two or three months before I was transferred to the minimum security prison.

This prison was just a laid back easy going prison. After about a week there. I had caught on to the routine and ways of the system there. The do's and don'ts in other words.

I had written some ten songs by now. I began to sing them at the chapel when we had a service. The prisoners really liked them. It also impressed the Chaplain and the guards.

The Chaplin made away for me to be able to come out to the Chapel and stay all day. I would sit and write songs. Hum new tunes. And write new words. One day I wrote Kenneth Hagin about a Bible Course.

He wrote me back and told me something about my letter sparked him. He said he prayed over my letter and felt lead of God to send me the very same course that he offers to his students at Rhema Bible College. Free of charge. It was a three year study on the Bible and ways of the Bible.

I began taking those lessons. The Chaplin let me come to the Chapel to study. Where it was quite. One day the Chaplin told me he was going to check me out of prison and let me go visit his wife and their home. He like to make things out of wood and stuff.

He said I had to promise him that I wouldn't try and run away. I said I would never do that. I told him how so much that prison was helping to put my life back together. That running was totally out of the question.

That was great day for me. The Chaplin owned a 1932 Ford restored Truck and a 1932 restored Ford car. Man they were sharp. I drew him a picture of his truck after that day. It surprised him very much. He was thrilled. His wife was also.

But that was just my way of saying Thank You for being my friend.

Here are a couple more songs I wrote while I was at the minimum security prison. The Chaplin really could tell something was going on in my life. It was, it was God.

You Found Me MDW 01-16-1989

As I look back at the things I've done.
I'm so ashamed I feel I want to run.
I was deep in sin how did You find me?
And rescue me from this cold sea.

Thank You Lord You seen away to save me.
You led me out of deaths stormy sea.
Thank You Lord what else can I do?
Only praise You and tell others to.

Dear Lord You came and You found me.
You picked me up from this cold black sea.
You were the light in the darkness.
Now Lord I give You all my praises.

==

Since Jesus Came My Way MDW May 1991

In my life of pain and strife.
I was going the wrong way.
I was so confused.
I didn't have any night or day.
But then the Lord came by.
To show me the way.
I found a new and better day.
When Jesus came my way.

Since Jesus came my way.
No more darkness is in my day.
I can see ahead.
By the love that He spread.
He took my cloudiness away.
He took my burdens that day.
Since Jesus came my way.
I've had a new and better day.

I found a new and better day.
When Jesus came my way.
He took me out of sin.
And placed His love within.
Now my future is so bright.
And my day is no more night.
I found a new and better day.
When Jesus came my way.

One day the Chaplin came to me and told me he had some bad
news for me. He told me my oldest brother had been killed in a car
accident. Oh how my heart fell to my feet at that very instant. He
was one of the motivations I had to learn all that I had learned. I
was going to help him get off alcohol. He never had a drug issue.
But he did have a sever alcohol problem.

I felt robbed. My brother could pick a guitar very well. It came
natural to him. I was going to get with him after I got out of prison
and see if we couldn't get a band started or something. Now the
devil had taken that away.

For a couple days there. I felt empty. I felt robbed. I felt all I had
learned was now for nothing. But then my mind came back to me. I
hadn't did it all for my brother. I hadn't did it all for anyone. Except
myself. I was the one needing that kind of treatment and help. Me
and only me. I began to feel better.

One day at the canteen. I waiting to buy some coffee. There was this skinny little guy there beside the canteen. There was three guards all around him. They were giving him a very hard time.

I had gained the respect of most all the guards by now. So that night this one guard was a minister. He was on duty. We began to talk about the Bible and things.

Then I ask him, "I saw today a couple of you guards giving this skinny guy a hard time." "Why is that?" I said, " You take this other guy. He runs a gambling game all the time. No one ever says a word about him. Then you find this skinny guy and you all hassle him to death." "Why is that?"

He answered me and said, "Well, you take the skinny guy. He has learned a lesson. He will probably never come back to prison. So we guards make sure he has learned that lesson and learned it well."

"The on the other hand. You take the guy that has the gambling game. He will never learn a lesson. Soon as he gets out of prison. He'll back into trouble again. So we leave him alone. He is job security. If everyone was like the skinny guy. We'd be out of a job. But thanks to people like the gambling guy. We'll always a job."

That made so much sense to me. I just smiled and walked away. I had about thirty books in my locker I was going to send home on visit day. I was sitting in the day room when this other guard ask me, "Can you stand a shake down?"

I told him, "Can you stand to shake me down?" I knew I didn't have anything to hide. He said, "Go bust it open." meaning to open my locker. So I did. He started out looking through my stuff looking for drugs or contraband.

He had been at it about an hour when all of a sudden. He just started placing books on the bed without looking through them. I said to him, "Hey, what you doing. The one you miss is the one that has the stuff in it." He just stopped and walked away.

He never ever even looked at me the rest of the time I was in prison. Another day I was laying on my bed this guard came by and grabbed the toe of my shoe and said, "come on." I ask him where we were going. He said, "outside to cut grass." I told him, "I ain't cutting no grass. I'm in here for a crime. Not to cut grass." He got someone else to cut the grass.

My final score with the Kenneth Hagin Bible study was a 98%. I got a diploma. I had already finished about five other Bible study lessons. The Chaplin told me he had a certificate for a three year resident Bible study course at Wheaton Bible College.

He said he had already sent my name in on it. I received the letter stating that I had a fully paid tuition including books, housing, food and all. All I had to do was to report at the college on the day stated on the letter. I had to find a job on the
campus. that would help off set some of the cost to the college.

But, I went out of the Will of God and didn't go. I had met this lady that came with her church to hold services on Saturday nights at the prison. She would come visit me on my regular visit days also.

It was close to time for me to be released from prison. I was transferred one last time to a prison close to my home town. I was only there about two weeks and then I was released from prison.

Chapter 5

Fresh New Ground

I kept seeing this girl. Then one day I moved in with her. Her sisters and her Mom kept asking when we were getting married. I wasn't planning on getting married. I was planning on going to Wheaton, Illinois to that Bible college.

I was thinking this was what God wanted me to do. I was living with this girl so that I wouldn't have to live with my Mom and Dad. The reason was, I didn't want to be there and my children show up. That may have caused a lot of undue bad feelings. Or emotional issues. So I was trying to avoid that.

One day this girls sister just flat out ask me, "Are you going to marry her or not?" So the next day we went to the court house in South Carolina and signed up to be married.

This girl was a good Christian girl. She was kind hearted. Gentle and sweet. She had passion, and compassion on every living thing. I didn't want her to get a bad reputation over me and her just living together unmarried.

The next day we went in the court house and stood in front of the judge. When he ask me if I took her to be my lawful wedded wife. I said, "I do." Just that fast, that very instant. I felt something inside of me. It raised up out of my belly and went out through my left shoulder. It pulled me as it exited my body.

I have always felt like it was God's Spirit that he had planted in me that night way back in the jail cell in 1988. Our troubles started almost immediately. We would fuss and be mad at each other all the time.

I didn't want to live like that. So I left. We were only married about six months when I left. I went to my Mom and Dad's home. I felt different. I was thinking different. Something had changed in me.

I began to go to different churches looking for one that matched the one my Bible lessons said the should be. But I just couldn't find one. Most all the churches I went to had spending money on the building of the church rather than the True Church of God, the people.

Plus some of the members and the pastor of some of the churches acted high and mighty. A better than you kind of attitude. Some of the pastors didn't even want to talk to you unless you had some sort of job to do in the church. That was no way to be.

I was thirty seven years old at this time. Living back with Mom and Dad. I still was not able to discuss any problems or issues I was having with them. Everytime I tried to explain something to them. They said, "Well, it'll get better." So I didn't even try. I had no minister to talk to.

Wasn't long until my youngest brother brought a camper up to my Dad's. He told me I could live in it if I hooked up the water and sewer and power. So I did. Shortly after that my brother and his wife separated. He came up to the camper to live with me.

My youngest brother plays a guitar very well. He can hear you sang a song and
before you get to the course of that song, he is picking it. So I got out the songs
that God had given to my mind to write. We would sit up almost until dawn picking and singing those songs.

Dad told me one day. He said, "I heard ya'll out there last night. Sounded pretty
good. I started to come out and join ya'll." It would have been great if he had. But,
my brother drank beer. Dad is totally against any kind of alcohol.

Dad and Mom are old fashioned Christian people. They don't believe in any drugs other than what a doctor prescribes. No alcohol of no kind at anytime. No cussing or by words at anytime. Plus a lot of other stuff.

Wasn't long until my brother and his wife reconciled. He gave me the camper.
I met this lady. I knew her from her sister. Her sister and the brother that is one year younger than me, used to live together.

We dated for about six months. She has two grown children. Her two children likes to take advantage of her. They grew up with out their Dad around. He never came to visit them or anything. They grew up telling their Mom what to do.

When I got involved with their Mom. They didn't like to good. I told both of them one day, "When I move in with your Mom. There's going to be some drastic changes." I told them, "Your gonna call me Dad!" They said, "No we won't!"

I did move in with her. I did make some drastic changes. I made her stop giving those grown up men her money. She wound up buying for herself a new living suit. A new bedroom suit. A kitchen table and chairs plus a nice hutch for dishes.   We lived together for four years. Then she had a baby, in 1997. I was forty two years old.

After my son was born. God was still working on me and for me. It had been eleven years since I last saw any of my children from my second marriage. I had never hurt or abused or anything to my boys. But after I got out of prison I didn't want to cause any conflicts or commotions by trying to contact them I just figured that when the time was right and all was well. They would contact me.

One day sitting at the window. My oldest son walked upon the porch. He knocked on the door. He said, "I heard I got a new brother." I said, "You have." We had a wonderful visit. He told me he missed me a lot. I told him I thought about him everyday.

I apologized for the things I had done. He forgave me. So we started building our relationship back from that moment. I had been helping my younger brother remodel his home. I had started back drinking beer.

My youngest son wasn't so easy. He and a couple of his friends came to see me one day and jumped on me. They didn't actually beat me up. But my son did punch me in the mouth.

I wasn't mad. I felt I deserved that. For what I had done to his sister. I also thought, a small price to pay. Wasn't long after that. Here comes their Mom and a about three or four men. They just burst right in and jumped on me. When they left. I went and took out an assault charge on her.

When It went to court. I told the judge what had happened. I also told the judge the reason it happened. Because I had done what I done to her daughter, my daughter. I also told the judge I had paid my price to society and I deserve to live peacefully. I also told the judge that I had never tried to contact my daughter or my sons or their Mom in no way shape or form. Not by phone, not by letter, not by friend. No way at all.

The judge ordered her to stay away from me. He told her that if she as much as looks at me in a store he will put her in jail for five years. I've not had any type problem out of her since.

It took a couple more years. But one day, my youngest son came around. He apologized for what he done. I apologized for what I had done. Soon it was just water under the bridge. It was God working out my issues.

Then one day my oldest son and my nephew came to the house. They wanted me to go with them to the game room and shoot some pool. I told them I didn't want to go. That I had been drinking beer all day. But they just kept on. Then my nephew spoke up and said, "The owner of the game room don't mind if you drank.
He has probably got some there right now. As long as you play his games. He'll give you beer." Right then I said, "Well, let's go."

We walked into the game room. There was this man and his girl playing pool. My nephew puts up quarters for next game. Meaning he would take on the winner of that game. I just slid upon a bar stool. My son was just walking around.

It came time for my nephew to play the winner of that game. So they began. My son said to my nephew, "Beat him now so we can get control of the table. I want to play Dad." My nephew said, "I do to."

My nephew won. So it was my nephew and my sons turn to play. Both of them were ragging on me, about wanting to beat me at pool. I was taught by a couple well know pool sharks. Ole three finger Joe. And Albert Anderson.

I used to shoot a mean stick. But it had been probably over twenty five years since I shot any serious pool. I had drank maybe two of the owners beers by now. Suddenly, the door opens. In walks four guys. They were loud and cutting up. Now,
I am an old hand at running to bars and clubs. I know trouble. My instincts told me right off this was trouble coming in. So I slid of the bar stool and went to the rest room. I was wanting to splash water on my face to sober up all I could.

I could hear inside the rest room that a commotion had broken out between somebody. When I came out of the rest room I rounded the corner. Everyone was going out side. So I also went out side. When I walked out, there was four guys all lined up in a row side by side. I saw my nephew and my son lined up side by side in front of the four guys. All facing each other.

I walked out beside my son and took my stand. I wanted to even the odds up some. I never said a word. All of a sudden the tallest on of the four. Comes out and POW! My son falls straight back. I thought the guy had knocked my son out. But soon as he did that. All the four guys took off running in the opposite direction. I knelt down to check on my son. He was dead. Shot in the head right above his eyes.

I was in shock. We had just got back together as son and Dad about 3 months before this happened. The devil robbed me again. Wasn't long after that. The girl that had my last son. Well we got to where we couldn't get along anymore. She had some mental issues that sprouted after our son was born. I just couldn't handle it.

We still see each other. She still calls me her boyfriend. Our son is thirteen now. He does very well in school. I am very happy about that. But I can't help but to think about my oldest son everyday. Especially on our birthday. We shared the same birthday.

I wrote this for him:

'Today' April 28, 2007

The rains came slowly today, as I thought of you.
I wasn't able to go outside, so my mind took a wondering view.
It bounced from here, and bounced to there, from one on to the other. Then came you and your wonderful smile, and, us laughing together. We did have some fun times, full of joy, and carefree cheer. I think of them often, you and me, year after year after year.
We did have some bad times, as everyone does you know.
But we pulled through, slow and strong, just rolling with the flow.
I remember sometimes, people would ask me, " Where's you shadow today"? I'd just laugh and tell them smiling, "The clouds hasn't yet gone away". I remembered all the first times, I got to give to you. Like when we went on top of the mountain, and saw the splendid view. And down to the beach I'll never forget, those words you used to describe it. " Just looks like a big lake to me, how'd the salt get in it"? Yes, the rains came slowly today, as I thought of you. Dripping down on my paper, I'm missing you ever so true.

in memory of my son, Steven. 1975-1997

In the year 2000. I went up to my Dad's to help him work on his car. I lay down on my back to look under the car. When I sat up, I got so dizzy I almost passed out. I just brushed it off as lack of food or getting over drinking the day before. I never said anything to Dad or anyone else.

After about a month. I was beginning to get very tired when I walked or did much of anything. Then I began hurting in my chest. I went to the doctor. He did some test on me. Then he told me he was sending me to a heart doctor.

The heart doctor did some test on me. He said I had a clotted artery. He wanted to do this procedure where he takes a thing and goes into the leg artery and runs it up to the clot and burst it into pieces to unclog the artery. I sad ok. Well I went for this. The doctor ran that thing up my right leg with no progress. So he ran it up my left leg with no progress. He said he didn't know what was wrong.

So he scheduled me for another heart doctor to look at me. He was a specialist on the heart. This doctor told me that I needed open heart surgery. He said I had, had a massive heart attack. He said that when I had the heart attack, that my artery had exploded. But at the very instant it exploded. It fussed itself back together at the same time on both open ends.

He said they needed to go in there and piece together that artery. Because my heart wasn't getting enough blood to it. He also said in his forty years as a heart surgeon he has never seen anything like that happen before. He said I was a first. He also told me if that other doctor had a gotten that instrument to break through what he thought was a clog. I would have died.

So I went ahead and let him do the surgery. Man the next day I woke up. I felt brand new. I still had an IV in my arm. But I needed and wanted a cup of coffee. So I ask the nurse. But she never brought me one. Then I remembered a waiting room on the floor below where I was. They had make your on coffee there.

I just grabbed that pole holding the IV bag and off I went to the elevator. I went down to the floor below and I got a hand full of that instant coffee. Then I went back to my floor. The nurses were all going wild. They said, "Where did you go?" I told them. they said I was on a monitor being watched just in case something went wrong about my heart. They said all sorts of buzzers and bells went off. They said I had flat lined.

Those nurses told me not to leave off that floor any more. I said I wouldn't. The
doctor told me after I was in the hospital two days that I was doing so well. That I
could go home if I wanted to. He also said he would suggest I stay until Monday.
He said it would give him the opportunity to know everything went as planed.

But hey, I wanted out of there. So I left. But I really wish I had a stayed. When I
got home. I picked up a flu virus. I had it bad. I couldn't hear anything. A roaring in my head was so loud. I was coughing so deep and hard. My head felt like it was full of jello.

I went to the bath room. I slipped and fell. I hurt my self a lot worse than I first
thought. That night I wasn't able to get to the bath room. I was hurting so bad in my chest. I couldn't even walk from the head of my bed to the foot of my bed with out having to stop and rest.

I took an ACE bandage and wrapped it around my chest to give me some relief
from all the pain I was having. The next day I went to the emergency room. But they just told me I needed to call my heart surgeon. They brushed it off as just chest pains from my surgery.

I called the heart surgeon. But the nurse on charge told me that the doctor was
scheduled for surgery for the next thirty days and he wouldn't be able to see me. So I was stuck. But after about two weeks. The pain had gotten so bad I just couldn't take it anymore.

So I called the heart doctor back and explained my situation to them. They said
they could let me see a different doctor. I told them I didn't care I needed someone to check me out.

I went over there. Soon as I got there. They took me back for x-rays. All of a
sudden the doctor came in and scheduled me for emergency surgery.

When I fell. I broke all but one of the steel ties that held my breast bone together to heal after my open heart surgery. It also broke two of my bottom ribs off. The doctors had to remove the two ribs. They also has reconstruct my breast bone using some sort of plastic. They had to place two titanium rods in there and bolt my breast bone and ribs to the rods.

The doctor told me that if that last band had a broken. All my innards would have
gushed out into my chest and I would have died instantly. He said the ACE bandage I wrapped around me help in saving my life. It help keep that last band from breaking. He also told me my working days were over. That I couldn't pick up any thing over ten pounds. He said if I did. It would force the screws out of place. Then there would be another set of issues to have to deal with.

So that put me on disability. All that has robbed me of most of my energy. It's hard for me now to walk any distance at all. I have to sit down and rest when I sweep my floor now. My regret is, I can't run and chase after my son. I cant play ball with him. I can't go mountain climbing with him. I can't swim with him.

But he understands. But I can tell he wishes I could. I wish I could also. My
youngest son. Now there is a character. He doesn't listen to his Mom much. But he
listens to everything I say.

But his Mom let's him get by with things, I don't. He more or less tells his Mom
what to do. What to cook. Where to go. What to watch on TV. Just everything. He
tried that with me. But I put him in his place. I told him, "Your not my Dad. I'm your
Dad. I don't do as you say. You do as I say."

Plus his Mom has never disciplined him on anything. I have. I have taken his play
station away. But over all. He is a well behaved boy. Gets good grades at school.
Has a lot of nice friends. He's is kind just like his Mom. He also tender hearted like
his Mom.

It was 2008. My Dad told me that my daughter had come to work at the Hardee's where we ate breakfast a lot of mornings. I told my Dad, "Well, I guess we'll just have to find some other place to have breakfast."

He said, "No, she wants to see you. God was working again on my behalf. It had been twenty years since I last saw my daughter. But, I also didn't want to cause any conflicts or problems or any mental issues or anything like that.

I was in to bad of shape for any kind of bad stuff to go on. Plus I didn't want to

inflict any more pain upon my daughter than I had already done in the past. I waited for a couple days and thought about it over and over in my mind. I ask God what would be better for me to do.

After a couple days. Dad brought me a note from my daughter. The note said, "I

want to see you. I have some things to tell you. Call me." And it gave her phone

number.

I had my answer from God right there. So I called Dad that night. We went to

Hardee's the next morning. There was my daughter working. She looked up and saw me. She came running around the counter and grabbed me and hugged me right there.

It was so amazing. When things slowed down some. She came over to our table

and we began to talk a little. I told her where I lived. I ask her to please not come if

she was going to cause me trouble or problems. She promised that, that was not

her intentions.

She came over. We had a great and wonderful talk. I apologized to her. For all that I had done to her. She said she had forgiven me a long time ago. She said she had been trying to get in touch with me. But no one would tell her where I lived or give her my phone number.

I told her that, that was people looking out for my safety and things. Because of

what her Mom and her brother had done in the past. I had written a song in 1993

about her. I had recorded it. I had a chance to give it to her. It made her cry. Here is that song:

There's A Thorn MDW 04-16-1993

Just a rose, in this garden of time,
tiny pedals there all mine.
But the storms came,
and broke you down.
Now all I have,
is this thorn now.

There's a thorn I carry now.
No one knows the pain I have.
They won't let those memories die.
There's a thorn I carry now.

Some people say your budding again,
with lost memories and help from friends.
I'm so glad your worlds not torn,
as mine is with this thorn.

   My daughter and me have been building our relationship up ever
since. It has been wonderful. Just another thing showing how that
God loves me and wants to help me.
   I was always thinking I would never get to a chance to fully say I
was sorry for the things I had done to my daughter. I was also
thinking that my boys would never ever want to talk to me again for
the things I had done to their sister. I lived in constant wonderment. I
was never happy until my last son was born in 1997. That put my
mind to thinking in a different direction.

Today I live alone. I am disabled. I can't hardly walk. I have COPD a lung disease. God still brings to my mind a song now and again. I believe He let me write so many songs in prison was to help me pass my time away. To keep my mind on Him and not my circumstances.

I am by far not financially rich. But I am by far richer than most. Because what the devil took from me. God gave it all back to me and then more. I am single and I am going to stay that way.

I never could learn how to play an instrument. That just wasn't in God's plan for me or my family. God showed me one night in a dream. That my family was suppose to travel around and sing and make music. Sharing the Good news Of Jesus Christ. And sharing the Love of God with everyone.

That my Dad, my oldest brother. My youngest brother and next to the youngest
brother were to play guitars. My adopted brother which is really my nephew was
suppose to play he bass guitar. While my brother who is one year younger than me, and my self were to sing. As well as the whole family was suppose to sing. I was suppose to write what we sung.

But the devil worked his way in and took all that away. You can read about it in
my book titled: "The Divine Plan - Broken". You can also hear some of the music I wrote, my family put the music to at:

www.odds10to1.com

Here are some more of the thins that God gave to me:

A New Day 3-15-2008

As the dawn breaks a new day, peaceful, slumber fresh.
Tiny dew drops reflect the daylight.
As the birds sing their very own songs.
I watch the winds blow the tender leaves.
As I smell the soft breeze.
And I wonder what the day is going to be.
Even though the day may hold for me,
another lonely period of misunderstanding and unconcern's.
I still have beaten all odds at its best.
I awoke today to the sound of music,
calm, fresh, and content.

==

God and A Friend   09-04-2007

No greater love than the love of God,
but a real true friend runs a close second.
To know God and love God,
is to study and live by His Word.
To know and have a true friend,
is the means by which to accomplish.
Trust, care, correction, and acknowledgment,
come from both God and a true friend.
Understanding, forgiveness, and forgetfulness,
should also be a part of ones life.
For with-out God, it's a hopeless life.
With-out a true friend, it's a hopeless life.
Someone to brag to, someone to cry to,
someone to share with, someone to care with.
Someone to fight with, someone to make up with.
Someone like God and a friend.

God's Artistic Hand   MDW 03-18-2009

Well, I walked outside today, to the concrete slap in my yard.
I carried my old green plastic lawn chair, it was once tuff and hard.
I sat down under the big shade tree, coffee in my hand.
I began to see God's amazing artistry, so beautiful and grand.
I saw the bright warm sunshine, flickering between the leaves.
As they gently swayed back and forth in the gentle breeze.
I never knew there was so much different greens to behold.
Like grass, and leaves, and bushes, so different and untold.
I saw tiny flowers, yellow, pink, and white.
I saw large large red and purple ones, what a wondrous sight.
Different birds were singing, their very own song.
It all come together, as an orchestra soft and strong.
Squirrels were playing, chasing each other round the old tree.
Peace had finally found away to come to me.
I thought to myself, can Heaven be this way.
Is God giving me a glimpse, here on this day?
My eyes began to water, my nose began to run.
I started coughing, choking and gagging the dream was finally
done.
The old plastic chair leg, gave way to the action.
I fell on my knees with a mighty thump, and that chair attacking me
without any passion.
My allergies had kicked in, and I knew it time to go.
So I rose up in agony, and headed to the door so slow.
With two skint knees and broken chair, I hobbled to my home.
Still coughing, gagging and sneezing, and trying not to moan.
Satan always finds away to disrupt a good thing.

Happy Birthday Dear Jesus MDW November 1990

The faces are full of smiles, this time of year.
People are so anxious, to spread some love and cheer.
There's peace everywhere, and the air, is fresh and new.
Happy Birthday Dear Jesus, and Merry Christmas too.

Happy Birthday Dear Jesus, and Merry Christmas too.
I just took time to remember, this is all for You.
From the star on the tree, that Guided the wise men three.
To the presents they gave You, that's given to me.

Love is everywhere, for all to see.
Peace and joy, is in everything.
We owe it all to You, for all You have done.
Happy Birthday Dear Jesus, I'm so glad that You Come.

I Saw His Hands   MDW JUNE 1991

(1)
I began to see my life, all the troubles and the pain and strife.
I had no one who really cared for me.
I gave no reasons for love to share, or for anyone else to care.
Until I looked into my heart to see.

(cho)
I saw His hands and His feet, where Jesus died for you and me.
I saw the thorns upon His head, and the blood that He shed.
I saw the stripes upon His back, and I knew I was on the right track.
Because He loves me, yes, He really loves me.

(2)
I knew then that there was some hope, That Jesus Christ would help me
cope.
So I changed the way I was right then and there.
I looked deep into my heart, searching to be set apart.
And Jesus showed me, yes, He showed me.

===

I stepped outside this cool cloudy morning.
Coffee in my hand, a smoke in my lips.
Dew was on the grass, and on the flowers.
You came into my mind.
Three baby squirrels were chasing each other around the tree.
The birds were chirping like a symphony.
I feel a gentle breeze blow the smoke of my cigarette.
Then I thought, how lucky I am.
I'm far from rich, I don't have high dollar valuables.
I owe bills.
But I do have much more than most.
I have you as my Friend.

Victory MDW August 1989

I want to sing for Jesus for all He's done.
In my life and the time I run.
He never let me go totally.
I see now that He does love me.
From sins dark sea He lifted me.
Now I fight for my Savior for the victory.

People and things can't make me fall.
I look up to Jesus and He hears my call.
I have found a better way to live my life.
Although they try with the devil's hand.
The power of God is what helps me stand.
And through all of my strife I have the victory.

When the trumpet of the Lord sounds out.
And the Christians ascend in a shout.
I'll be in that number on my way to Glory.
All my troubles and pain will be through.
I'll have a Heavenly body all brand new.
and I'll have the power of God and the victory.

==

I'm Thankful For You MDW 11-15-2000

I'm Thankful for You,
and all You do.
All the whole year through.
I thank God for You,
I thank You too.
Without You,
I don't know what I would do.
Thank You.

I'm A Mis-Fit MDW October 1992

I've done things man can't forget.
They won't forgive.
But I regret.
That I've done wrong.
Christ forgave my every sin.
Jesus choose the mis-fits.
To spread His Word.
Every bit.
And Jesus chose me.
Because I fit.

I'm not perfect you see.
That's why Christ chose me.
To spread His Precious Word.
Every bit.
I said I'm sorry from my heart.
And Christ gave me a new start.
He loves because.
I'm a mis-fit.

Poor and needy, broke and bound.
That's who Christ, would hang around.
They got His attention, every bit.
Most very busy Christ would use.
To find their heart, for the truth.
But for love.
He always choose a mis-fit

Jousting for the Win MDW 10-11-2009

Riding around on my scooter one day,
I heard a train and it was headed my way.
Speeding up to cross the railroad track first,
suddenly it happened and it came with a burst.
The signal arm so mighty and so long,
came down with a vengeance and oh so strong.
Jousting me off my scooter like a Knight,
I was stunned, and shocked, and full of fright.
I hit the road with a mighty donk,
my scooter kept going like a wild bucking bronc.
My scruples were scattered and I was in disarray,
I really thought, I was dead that day.
Lying in the road as the train went by,
cars were a coming all I seen was the sky.
A Police man just happened to be near,
came to help, he too was in fear.
He said, "I saw the whole thing and that was quite a show."
"Now my boy, lets get you out of the road."
I couldn't hardly move I was so full of pain,
my scruples hadn't yet, returned to my brain.
Fighting for my breath and pain awfully,
I begged that Policeman to kill my agony.
He said, "All will be OK, an ambulance is on the way,"
"I'll take your scooter home so it'll be OK."
Now when I'm riding I come upon the train track,
my mind automatically takes me back.
To the day I played the Knight jousting for the win,
to beat that train, never again.

Me and The Rat   07-27-2010

Well I got an ole rat doing damage around the home.
I thought it simple to catch him, and then he'd be gone.
Turns out to be that rats smarter than I thought.
So a nice new trap, I up and went and bought.
First day on the job, that rat's playing hard ball.
He stole the bait, spoon and all.
I said to myself, "ok, fine and dandy."
I got a milk jug cap that I had real handy.
I wired that sucker down to the cage floor.
Baited it up and opened the door.
Woke up next day much to my dismay.
That rat had licked that cap clean and got away.
So I put a partition up to help erase.
Blocking out about 4 inches of space.
I removed the milk cap and replaced with a wire.
Looped and anchored hoping for my desire.
Much to my dismay that rat did it again.
He stole the bait and in his hole went in.
I'm beginning to think this rat is educated.
My smarts are becoming just a little faded.
Determined now to put and end to this task.
I put some plastic on the partition mask.
Waking the next day, I looked to see.
The door to the trap was tripped but was empty.
Frustrated and angered I said, "I'll get you."
So I sit down and thought just what to do.
 I put plastic on the sides and the back.
So that rat would have to go inside for a snack.
When I woke the next day I went to see,
That darn ole rat did it again, out smarted me.
So I brought the cage in and sit and studied awhile.
Then a thought come to me that made me smile.
I took some screws, some wire and a piece of steel,
I'll weight the door down, that'll stop his steal.
I woke the next day in hopes of a clutch.
That darned ole trap wasn't even touched.
Now I got to try something new.

Thank You for ordering and reading my book. I do hope it was able to give some insights into just how important communication with your children is.

If I had, had good communication with my parents. I may not have suffered as I did. I may have not made some of the decisions I did.

Nothing with-in these pages may be
copied or used by anyone in anyway
with out my written consent and seal

Copyright © 2010 Michael D. Wood

www.odds10to1.com

www.ingramcontent.com/pod-product-compliance
Lightning Source LLC
Chambersburg PA
CBHW062109280526
45788CB00003B/1401